A Guide to Selling your Business and Optimizing your Business Exit

How to Get the Most for selling your Business with less stress and Maximum Price

By

Lane J. Taylor

Copyright © 2024 by Lane J. Taylor. All rights reserved. ISBN:9798320490069. This book or any piece thereof may not be replicated or utilized by any stretch of the imagination using any means without the consent of the Writer/distributer except for the use of brief references in a book survey.

Disclaimer

The information contained within this book is intended solely for informational and educational purposes. The author, Lane J. Taylor, does not hold credentials as a financial advisor, and therefore, the strategies, insights, and recommendations provided should not be construed as professional financial, legal, or business advice. Readers are strongly encouraged to seek personalized guidance from qualified professionals tailored to their specific circumstances.

Neither the author nor the publisher make any representations or warranties regarding the accuracy, completeness, or suitability of the information presented herein. The use of any information from this book is at the discretion and risk of the reader. The author and publisher disclaim any liability for direct, indirect, incidental, consequential, or special damages arising from the use of this book or the information within.

It is crucial for readers to independently verify and evaluate the applicability of the strategies outlined in this book based on their individual situations. Any mention of specific products, services, or third-party websites is not to be construed as an endorsement or recommendation.

While efforts have been made to ensure the accuracy of the information at the time of writing, technological advancements and changes may have occurred since publication. The author has no affiliation with any third-party products or services mentioned and references are provided for illustrative purposes only. The success of any strategies or techniques is contingent upon various factors, and individual results may vary.

By reading this book, the reader acknowledges and agrees to the terms of this disclaimer. It is advisable to consult with appropriate professionals before making significant decisions based on the information presented herein.

About the Author

Renowned for his expertise in wealth-building principles and financial markets, Lane J. Taylor is recognized as a distinguished financial expert and dedicated researcher. Going beyond conventional finance, he explores the convergence of finance and technology, providing innovative insights. With a commitment to simplifying complex financial concepts, Taylor's research offers practical applications for accessible wealth creation. As a highly sought-after speaker, he shares actionable insights on investment strategies, technology, and the psychology of wealth. Taylor continues to stay ahead of the curve in financial and technological advancements, motivating others to discover the possibilities at the nexus of finance and technology for financial success.

Table of Contents

Introduction   7

Chapter 1:Contemplating on Selling Your Business   13

Chapter 2:Fully Understanding of the Process   33

Chapter 3: The People and Market   45

Chapter 4: Concerns from Sellers   55

Chapter 5: Bank and Financing Options   67

Chapter 6: Common pitfalls when selling the Business   73

Conclusion   83

Leaving a Review   87

Introduction

For those engrossed in the realm of business Life, it's evident that an abundance of resources exists to guide you through the process of launching a Business. From comprehensive guides on business initiation to detailed strategies on company expansion, product marketing, and personal development in salesmanship, the wealth of information seems limitless. With an extensive array of books, academic courses, online tutorials, and instructional videos at your disposal, the potential for learning appears boundless. However, when it comes to the intricate art of selling a business, the landscape shifts drastically, leaving aspiring sellers to navigate largely uncharted waters. Unlike the plethora of resources available for starting and growing a business, there's a notable scarcity of guidance and support for those seeking to sell their enterprise.

It's a reality that entrepreneurs typically receive education and guidance predominantly focused on two phases of the entrepreneurial journey: the inception and the growth stages. However, what often goes overlooked is the equally significant third phase: exiting the business. Regardless of how meticulously one plans their entrepreneurial trajectory, the inevitability of departure looms large. Whether it's a voluntary decision, a circumstance that compels departure, or an eventuality beyond one's control, the reality remains unchanged: at some juncture, the entrepreneur will part ways with their business. Whether you opt for a graceful exit, are compelled to step down, or even if circumstances dictate an unexpected departure, the fact remains that one day, the business will cease to be a part of your life.

I understand that amidst the hustle and bustle of managing your business and navigating life's myriad responsibilities, there are countless pressing matters vying for your attention. However, amidst the chaos, it's crucial to recognize that the most pivotal action you can undertake for the longevity and success of your enterprise is to begin preparing for your eventual exit now.

While the prospect of departing from your business may seem distant or inconsequential amidst the daily grind, the truth is that the transition is inevitable. It may not transpire tomorrow, next month, or even within the next couple of years, but rest assured, it will occur—and often sooner than anticipated. By initiating preparations early, you afford yourself the luxury of peace of mind, enabling you to rest easier at night knowing that you're actively laying the groundwork for a seamless departure when the time inevitably arrives.

Moreover, by commencing preparations in advance, you not only mitigate the stress and uncertainty typically associated with exiting a business, but you also open the door to embracing the process with a sense of anticipation and even enjoyment. Rather than viewing it as a daunting task looming on the horizon, you can approach your exit as a carefully orchestrated transition, allowing you to savor the journey and relish the opportunities that lie ahead.

Immerse yourself in this groundbreaking manual, which will provide you with comprehensive insights and step-by-step guidance necessary for successfully navigating the process of selling your company. Delve into its pages to uncover invaluable information and actionable strategies that will equip you with the knowledge and skills needed to embark on this transformative journey. Don't hesitate to dive in and explore the wealth of resources this guide has to offer.

Chapter 1

Contemplating on Selling Your Business

The majority of business owners working with a brokerage can be categorized into two groups. If you find yourself in the first group, the notion of selling your business may seem unfathomable. For so long, your business has been your pride and joy, absorbing your time, energy, and even your identity. However, despite the emotional attachment, you've reached a point where you're ready to explore new horizons. This decision can be fraught with difficulty, akin to parting ways with something deeply cherished.

On the other hand, if you belong to the second group of owners, your business has morphed into a rebellious teenager, resistant to your guidance and care. Your life revolves around catering to the whims of a business entity that fails to acknowledge your needs. Even brief respites are marred by crises and challenges, leaving you drained and longing for relief. In such instances, it becomes clear that it's time to relinquish the burden and allow someone else to shoulder the responsibility. The need for your business to transition to new ownership becomes increasingly urgent.

Both of these scenarios can evoke a sense of overwhelming pressure, potentially leaving the owner feeling immobilized. It's crucial to acknowledge that, regardless of circumstance, your departure from the company is inevitable, whether it's by your own volition or external factors. Taking the initial step to contemplate this transition was undoubtedly challenging. However, there's still a considerable amount of groundwork to cover. You must spearhead efforts towards an outcome that maximizes value and secures the optimal result for your company. Although it entails rigorous preparation and diligent effort, the rewards of your endeavors will undoubtedly justify the investment.

Life, along with its inhabitants, remains inherently unpredictable and beyond our full control. Interestingly, some of the most erratic and unrestrained individuals I've encountered happen to be entrepreneurs (after all, it takes one to recognize another, doesn't it?). Many entrepreneurs, myself included, once held firm beliefs that selling our businesses was out of the question or deemed it a distant prospect unworthy of consideration. While such notions may offer a sense of comfort, the reality is far less accommodating. Ultimately, the decision to part ways with our businesses is not entirely within our grasp. Every entrepreneur will inevitably bid farewell to their business, whether through a dignified exit or, quite literally, until their last breath.

You Need Exit Alternatives , Not an Exit Strategy
Many business brokers advocate for the immediate creation of an exit plan, a detailed blueprint outlining your departure from the company, including outcomes and timing. However, some less ethical brokers may profit by crafting elaborate, but unrealistic, exit plans. Contrary to popular belief, you may not need an exit plan just yet. What's crucial are exit options: premeditated strategies offering a sustainable route to success and readiness for unforeseen circumstances necessitating a swift departure.

For small to medium-sized businesses, there are only four potential outcomes to consider (excluding the possibility of involuntary closure): You offload the business to an external buyer.

1. You offload the business to an external buyer.

2. You maximize the company's profits, then close shop and move on when you've exhausted its resources.

3. You transfer ownership to a trusted employee.

4. You hand over the reins to a family member or trusted business associate.

Unless your goal is an immediate departure, there's no urgency in determining your preferred outcome. Nonetheless, it's wise to anticipate each of these four possibilities. This ensures readiness to address any unforeseen developments promptly and without undue stress.

Hopefully, someday far down the road, you'll create a concrete exit plan. However, until then, equip yourself with exit options. Delaying this step can lead to regret—I've encountered numerous business owners who postponed developing exit options, only to rue their decision later on.

Locating a Purchaser

One of the most common inquiries from business sellers revolves around how to locate a buyer. Unlike traditional methods such as newspaper classifieds or open houses, there isn't a straightforward approach for potential buyers to discover businesses on the market. Should owners resort to displaying signs in windows or advertising online? Are there alternative methods they may not be aware of? I've even heard of a business owner attempting to gift their company to a college student in exchange for future royalties—though I don't endorse this strategy.

One avenue for finding buyers is leveraging your existing industry connections. In tightly-knit sectors or those where mergers and acquisitions (M&A) are prevalent, like the wealth management industry, owners can discover potential buyers within their network. This may involve methods such as reverse cold-calling or obtaining introductions through mutual acquaintances.

For owners who prefer a hands-on approach, there are direct marketing options available, but it comes with significant risks. This includes advertising on business sales websites and cold-calling potential buyers. While it may yield results, this approach often overlooks a crucial segment of potential purchasers: individual buyers, who typically engage brokers and bankers first.

Get a Business Broker

You might be inclined to believe that you can locate a buyer independently, but that assumption may not hold true. While most owners possess extensive knowledge about operating their company, they often lack expertise in selling it. The most effective approach to finding buyers is typically through the assistance of business brokers or investment bankers. If your company's value is below $25 million, you're likely to engage a broker, whereas if it exceeds $25 million, an investment banker is more common. Both professionals serve the same purpose: identifying suitable buyers and facilitating the sale of the business. They generate competition for your deal through confidential advertising and marketing strategies that sellers typically cannot replicate on their own. In many instances, brokers have the ability to cultivate a market for the company that would not exist otherwise.

Distinguishing between locating a buyer and successfully completing a deal is crucial. It's worth noting that approximately half of all deals collapse even after a buyer is found, and owners lacking experience in business transactions may encounter challenges in this regard. For instance, the owners of a specific medical company found themselves in a desperate situation and sought assistance from a brokerage. Despite their attempts to sell the company independently and receiving some initial interest, they struggled to finalize a deal. After engaging our business brokerage, however, the company was sold within four months, surpassing the owners' expectations with a sale price 50 percent higher than anticipated, despite being on the market for four years prior.

Buyers tend to approach sellers without brokers differently, with some potentially taking advantage of the situation. Recognizing the absence of experienced deal negotiators, they may attempt to undervalue their offer or include unfavorable terms that could pose challenges for former owners in the future. On the other hand, certain buyers may be cautious about purchasing businesses lacking third-party representation, assuming such companies are of inferior quality. Engaging a broker can instill confidence in both parties that the sale is being conducted according to standard market practices.

Moreover, a broker plays a crucial role in confidentially marketing your company. If employees and customers become aware of the sale, there's a significant risk of them leaving, potentially leaving you with nothing to sell. Therefore, a broker's expertise in maintaining confidentiality is paramount.

So, Who Exactly are These Elusive Business Purchasers?

Many business owners aiming to sell often envision buyers as either larger corporations or private equity firms. There's a certain allure to the idea of wealthy experts recognizing the value of your life's work. However, in truth, these types of buyers are in the minority. Regardless of the buyer's identity, your goal is to identify the "most probable buyer"—the one willing to offer the highest price, facilitate the smoothest deal, and leave the most positive legacy for your company.

Various entities are interested in acquiring companies:

Internal - You may opt to sell your business to someone already familiar with your industry, such as your general manager, offspring, or business partner. These buyers offer the advantage of preserving the company's legacy as they are already acquainted with its ethos. However, such deals may pose financial hurdles if the buyer struggles to provide a sufficient down payment or secure full financing, potentially prolonging the process. Additionally, this type of sale often involves emotional complexities that can complicate negotiations.

Even successful sellers typically receive interest from only a small number of potential buyers, and that's perfectly acceptable. Ultimately, the most suitable buyer is the one who successfully concludes the transaction. It's beneficial to identify as many potential buyers as possible and assess them based on your preferred transaction criteria. Remember, expanding the pool of potential buyers enhances competition for your business, increasing the likelihood of a successful sale and maximizing the selling price.

Individuals These individuals are usually seasoned business professionals with extensive corporate experience. They harbor a long-standing aspiration to own their own business and have concluded that purchasing an existing one is a more viable strategy than launching their own venture. Individual buyers comprise approximately 80 percent of business buyers. Unfortunately, many sellers, fixated on the fantasy of a private equity firm showering them with a windfall, initially overlook this demographic. However, doing so is risky; it's highly probable that your eventual buyer will be one of these individuals, and they are likely to offer you a more favorable deal than any other alternative.

Private Equity-PE Investor groups are individuals seeking to acquire a business, nurture its growth over a span of three to seven years, and eventually sell it at a premium. They typically target companies with annual EBITDA exceeding $1 million. Given that only 4 percent of US companies achieve revenue surpassing $1 million annually, these buyers are focusing on less than 1 percent of the market. Moreover, they exhibit specific preferences regarding industry, growth potential, owner involvement, and organizational personnel. Private equity firms (PE) often propose deal structures that transfer the risk back to the seller and may attempt to modify terms close to the deal's completion. In general, deals involving private equity firms tend to be disadvantageous for sellers.

Strategic/Synergistic These buyers typically consist of businesses that are either direct competitors or operate within a closely related industry, where merging with your company would enhance its growth potential. Often, they originate from different geographic regions or markets and aim to expand into yours. Typically, these companies are slightly larger than yours, with revenues ranging from 30 to 70 percent higher. It's important to dispel the notion that a large billion-dollar corporation will acquire your business, which generates revenues of $1 to $2 million. Multinational firms typically have extensive M&A divisions, and they require a significantly larger EBITDA (earnings before interest, taxes, depreciation, and amortization) for consideration.

Flippers -Indeed, they are real, and yes, their modus operandi resembles that of house flippers. These buyers seek out companies where they can leverage their unique skill sets to enhance value, intending to sell within one to three years. While they may not offer the highest prices, they act swiftly, making them appealing to sellers who value efficiency. Moreover, these flippers are willing to exert significant effort to revitalize struggling companies, making them an attractive option for sellers facing challenging circumstances.

What Could Make Someone Interested in Acquiring My Business?

When you first entertained the idea of selling your business, the initial question that likely crossed your mind was, "What is my business truly worth?" Unfortunately, there's no straightforward answer. Despite the abundance of information available online—surprising, I know—there isn't a universally reliable method for most individuals to determine a business's value. It's a blend of intuition and analysis, an amalgamation of art and science. Regardless of the number of rules of thumb you apply, online calculators you consult, or industry experts you seek advice from, accurately predicting a fair price that both a willing buyer and seller agree upon in neutral market conditions remains challenging. Ultimately, you'll obtain an accurate valuation only when you engage a business broker and officially list your company for sale. Until that moment, many owners reside in a realm of conjecture when contemplating the value of their business.

The allure of your business extends far beyond its tangible assets and financial metrics. While you may be preoccupied with determining its monetary value, potential buyers are drawn to a myriad of factors that transcend mere dollars and cents. From its loyal customer base and strong brand reputation to its innovative products or services and strategic market positioning, your business represents a unique opportunity for growth, expansion, and long-term success.

In the eyes of prospective buyers, your business embodies untapped potential, offering the promise of future prosperity and value creation. Whether it's a strategic investor seeking to capitalize on synergies and market opportunities or an aspiring entrepreneur eager to embark on their own journey of success, the appeal of acquiring your business lies in its ability to serve as a catalyst for growth, innovation, and profitability.

Moreover, beyond its intrinsic value, your business holds immense sentimental significance for potential buyers. It represents a labor of love, a testament to your vision, passion, and perseverance in bringing your entrepreneurial dreams to fruition. For some buyers, the opportunity to steward and build upon the legacy of your business is a compelling proposition—one that resonates deeply with their own aspirations and values.

Ultimately, the value of your business transcends mere numbers; it lies in its ability to inspire, empower, and transform the lives of those who dare to envision its potential. As you contemplate the prospect of selling your business, remember that its true worth cannot be quantified solely in monetary terms, but rather in the impact it has made and the opportunities it holds for the future.

Chapter 2

Fully Understanding of the Process

Selling a business isn't just about selling something—it's like embarking on a life-changing adventure. You have to plan every step carefully, think ahead strategically, and pay attention to even the smallest details. It's a journey where every move counts, starting from the moment you first consider selling to the final agreement handshake. Mastering how to sell your business means knowing how to navigate through all the important steps, each one playing a crucial role in making sure the sale is a big success and brings you the best possible outcome financially.

Step-by-Step Guide to Mastering the Business Sale Process

So, you've decided to sell your business. It's a big decision, but with the right approach, it can be a rewarding journey. Let's break it down into manageable steps to make sure you're fully prepared for what lies ahead.

First things first, preparation is key. Take a good, hard look at your business—its finances, operations, and market position. Figure out what's working well and what could use some improvement. This is your chance to spruce things up and make your business as appealing as possible to potential buyers.

Next, assemble your dream team. You're going to need some backup for this journey—legal experts, financial advisors, maybe even a business broker. Surround yourself with people who know the ins and outs of selling a business and can guide you through the process.

Once you've got your team in place, it's time to get the word out. Develop a marketing strategy to showcase your business to the world. Create compelling marketing materials, target the right audience, and get the word out through various channels. You want to drum up as much interest as possible to attract potential buyers.

When the inquiries start rolling in, it's negotiation time. This is where things can get a bit tricky, but don't worry—you've got this. Negotiate with potential buyers to hammer out the details of the deal, from price to terms to timelines. Stay flexible, but also stand firm on what's important to you.

As negotiations progress, be prepared for due diligence. Potential buyers are going to want to dig deep into your business to make sure everything checks out. Provide them with all the information they need, answer their questions honestly, and maintain transparency throughout the process.

Finally, it's time to seal the deal. Work with your legal and financial advisors to finalize the agreement, transfer ownership, and ensure a smooth transition for everyone involved. Take a deep breath, pat yourself on the back, and know that you've successfully navigated the business sale process like a pro.

So, there you have it—a step-by-step guide to selling your business like a seasoned pro. With careful preparation, strategic planning, and the right support team by your side, you can navigate the complexities of selling your business with confidence and achieve the best possible outcome.

How to Navigate Legal, Financial, Administrative Procedures for Goal Achievement

The legal procedures when selling your business is crucial to reaching your goals smoothly and securely. Here's a human-friendly breakdown of how to handle these steps:

1. Get Expert Advice: Start by reaching out to experienced legal professionals who specialize in business sales. They'll guide you through the legal maze and ensure you're on the right track with all the legal requirements.

2. Do a Legal Check-up: Before diving into the sale, take time to review your business's legal health. Look out for any potential issues like ongoing lawsuits, contracts, or compliance matters that might need addressing before moving forward.

3. Gather Your Paperwork: Collect all the necessary legal documents related to the sale, such as contracts, financial records, and intellectual property documents. Having everything organized and ready to go will save time and headaches later on.

4. Write Clear Contracts: Work closely with your legal team to draft clear and comprehensive contracts that outline all the terms of the sale. Make sure everything is spelled out clearly to avoid any confusion or misunderstandings down the road.

5. Be Prompt with Due Diligence: When potential buyers start asking for information during due diligence, respond promptly and provide all the requested documents. Being transparent and cooperative during this process builds trust and keeps things moving smoothly.

6. Negotiate Wisely: Negotiating the terms of the sale is a big part of the legal process. Work closely with your legal team to negotiate terms that protect your interests while still being fair to the buyer.

7. Stay Compliant: Throughout the process, make sure you're following all the relevant regulations and laws. Compliance is key to avoiding any legal hiccups that could derail the sale.

8. Close with Confidence: Once all the negotiations are done and everything's in order, work with your legal team to finalize the sale agreement and close the deal. Make sure all the paperwork is properly signed and that ownership of the business is transferred smoothly.

Also the financial and administrative side of selling your business smoothly and effectively is crucial to reaching your goals. Here's how to handle these aspects in a way that's easy to understand:

Financial Procedures:

1. Know Your Finances: Start by taking a close look at your business's financial situation. Review your financial statements, like your profit and loss statement, to understand where your company stands financially.

2. Figure Out How Much Your Business is Worth: Work with financial experts to determine the value of your business. They'll look at things like your assets, revenue, and growth potential to come up with a fair price.

3. Get Your Financial Documents in Order: Gather all the financial paperwork potential buyers might want to see, like your tax returns and balance sheets. Make sure everything is up-to-date and organized so you can present it easily.

4. Be Honest and Open: When it comes to money, transparency is key. Be prepared to answer questions from potential buyers honestly and provide them with all the information they need to make an informed decision.

Administrative Procedures:

1. Make a To-Do List: Create a checklist of all the administrative tasks you need to take care of during the sale process. This might include things like gathering documents or coordinating meetings with your team.

2. Share the Load: Don't try to do everything yourself. Delegate tasks to your team members or advisors to make sure everything gets done on time and correctly.

3. Stay Organized: Keep all your paperwork and communications organized and easy to find. You can use tools like cloud storage or project management software to help you stay on top of things.

4. Keep Everyone in the Loop: Communication is key. Make sure everyone involved in the sale process knows what's going on and what they need to do next.

5. Follow the Rules: Make sure you're following all the necessary rules and regulations throughout the sale process. This might include things like getting the right permits or licenses or making sure you're compliant with tax laws.

6. Prepare for the Transition: As the sale gets closer, start preparing for the transition of ownership. Make sure all your administrative records are up-to-date and ready to hand over to the new owner.

44

Chapter 3

The People and Market

In the journey of selling a business, people and the market both play crucial roles, each shaping the process in their unique way.

Role of People

Think of people as the driving force behind the sale. You've got your team of experts—legal advisors, financial gurus, and business brokers—all working together to make sure everything goes smoothly. They provide guidance, expertise, and support every step of the way, ensuring that the sale is a success.

But it's not just about your team; it's also about how potential buyers perceive them. Buyers aren't just looking at the business; they're also sizing up the people representing it. A strong, reliable team inspires confidence in buyers, making them more likely to seal the deal.

Clear communication and trust are key. When everyone involved is on the same page and trusts each other, negotiations go more smoothly, and everyone comes out happy in the end.

And let's not forget about the employees and stakeholders of the business. Keeping them in the loop and maintaining positive relationships with them is crucial during the sale process. After all, they're the ones who help make the business what it is.

Role of the Market

The market sets the stage for the sale. It's all about supply and demand—how many buyers are out there, and how attractive is your business to them?

A strong market can drive up demand for your business, leading to a higher sale price. But if the market isn't so great, you might have to adjust your strategy and expectations accordingly.

That's where market research comes in. By keeping an eye on market trends and what your competitors are up to, you can position your business effectively and make sure you're getting the best deal possible.

So, in the end, selling a business is all about understanding the people involved—your team, the buyers, and everyone else—and knowing how to navigate the market to your advantage. With the right people and a good grasp of the market, you're well on your way to a successful sale.

In order to facilitate an effective business selling process, one must build a support network and communicate effectively to the stakeholders.

Below are the steps to do so:

Building a Strong Support Network:

1. Assemble the Right Team: Surround yourself with a team of trusted professionals, including legal advisors, financial experts, and business brokers. Their expertise and guidance will be invaluable throughout the sale process.

2. Seek Mentorship: Connect with experienced entrepreneurs or business owners who have gone through similar exits. Their insights and advice can help you navigate challenges and make informed decisions.

3. Lean on Your Personal Network: Don't underestimate the power of your personal network. Friends, family, and colleagues can provide emotional support, encouragement, and valuable connections that can facilitate the sale.

4. Invest in Relationships: Build strong relationships with your team, advisors, and other key stakeholders. Trust and open communication are essential for fostering a collaborative and supportive environment.

Communicating Effectively with Stakeholders:

1. Be Transparent: Keep stakeholders informed about your plans to sell the business and the progress of the sale process. Transparency builds trust and minimizes uncertainty.

2. Address Concerns Proactively: Anticipate and address any concerns or questions that stakeholders may have about the sale. Providing clear and honest answers demonstrates your commitment to their interests.

3. Listen Actively: Take the time to listen to the concerns and feedback of stakeholders. Understanding their perspectives and priorities can help you tailor your communication and address their needs more effectively.

4. Provide Regular Updates: Keep stakeholders updated on important developments and milestones throughout the sale process. Regular communication ensures everyone is on the same page and reduces the likelihood of misunderstandings.

5. Maintain Confidentiality: While transparency is important, it's also essential to maintain confidentiality, especially during the early stages of the sale process. Ensure that sensitive information is shared only with those who need to know.

By building a strong support network and communicating effectively with stakeholders, you can navigate the challenges of selling a business with confidence and ensure a smooth exit for all involved parties.

Additionally you should also position yourself strategically to attract minimum interest and achieve the Maximum Price. This is like preparing a delicious dish – it requires the right ingredients and careful planning to attract the right attention and get the best price when it's time to sell.

1. Highlight What Makes You Special: Think about what makes your business unique. Maybe it's your top-notch customer service, your innovative products, or your unbeatable location. Whatever it is, make sure to shout it from the rooftops to grab the attention of potential buyers.

2. Keep Up with the Times: Stay in the loop about what's happening in your industry. Are there any new trends or technologies that could give your business a competitive edge? By staying ahead of the curve, you'll make your business even more appealing to buyers.

3. Show Off Your Finances: Just like you'd show off your best dishes to guests, showcase your business's financial performance. Share your revenue, profits, and growth projections to give buyers confidence in the value of your business.

4. Treat Your Customers Right: Your customers are like your biggest fans – they can make or break your reputation. Make sure to keep them happy and engaged, as their loyalty can add significant value to your business in the eyes of buyers.

5. Streamline Your Operations: Just like a well-oiled machine, your business should run smoothly and efficiently. Look for ways to cut costs, streamline processes, and improve performance to make your business even more attractive to buyers.

6. Build a Strong Brand: Think of your brand as your business's personality – it should be memorable, trustworthy, and appealing. Invest in building a strong brand identity and reputation to stand out in the marketplace and command a higher price.

7. Embrace Innovation: Innovation is like adding a secret ingredient to your recipe – it can take your business to the next level. Stay open to new ideas, technologies, and ways of doing things to keep your business fresh and exciting.

8. Get the Word Out: Just like you'd spread the word about your delicious dishes, make sure to promote your business far and wide. Use a mix of online and offline marketing tactics to reach potential buyers and generate interest in your business.

Making use of the above steps will not only attract maximum interest but also achieve the maximum price when it's time to sell. It's all about putting your best foot forward and making your business irresistible to buyers.

Chapter 4

Concerns from Sellers

Business owners considering a sale often have common concerns and queries as they navigate this significant decision. Addressing these concerns proactively can help ease anxieties and provide clarity throughout the process.

Valuation - One of the primary concerns for business owners is understanding the value of their business and whether they can achieve their desired sale price. Address this by conducting a thorough business valuation, considering factors such as financial performance, market conditions, and growth potential. Engage with experienced professionals to help determine a realistic valuation and develop strategies to maximize the sale price.

Confidentiality - Maintaining confidentiality is crucial to protect the business's reputation and prevent disruptions to operations during the sale process. Assure business owners that confidentiality measures will be in place, such as non-disclosure agreements with potential buyers and limited dissemination of sensitive information. Emphasize the importance of discretion and professionalism throughout the process.

Timing - Business owners may be uncertain about the optimal timing for a sale, fearing they might miss out on potential opportunities or sell prematurely. Provide guidance based on market trends, industry forecasts, and the business's readiness for sale. Consider factors such as financial performance, growth prospects, and personal circumstances to determine the most opportune time to sell.

Transition Planning - Concerns about transitioning out of the business and ensuring its continuity post-sale are common among business owners. Address these concerns by developing a comprehensive transition plan that outlines roles, responsibilities, and timelines for the transition period. Engage key stakeholders, including employees, customers, and suppliers, to facilitate a smooth transition and minimize disruptions to business operations.

Tax Implications - Business owners may have questions about the tax implications of selling their business and how to optimize their financial outcome. Offer guidance on tax planning strategies, such as structuring the sale to minimize tax liabilities and leveraging available tax incentives or exemptions. Encourage business owners to consult with tax advisors to ensure they fully understand the tax implications and explore all available options.

Legacy and Impact - Emotional considerations, such as preserving the business's legacy and ensuring its positive impact on employees and the community, are important for many business owners. Assure them that their legacy will be honored and that efforts will be made to find a buyer who shares their values and vision for the business's future. Highlight the potential benefits of the sale, such as providing opportunities for growth and innovation under new ownership.

Insightful Answers and Guidance to Sellers' Top Questions:

What is my business worth?

- Conduct a comprehensive business valuation, considering factors such as financial performance, market conditions, and industry trends.

 - Engage with experienced professionals, such as business appraisers or financial advisors, to determine a realistic valuation range.

  - Understand that the final sale price may vary depending on negotiations with potential buyers and market demand.

How can I maximize the sale price of my business?

   - Focus on increasing profitability and reducing costs to improve the business's financial performance.

  - Enhance the attractiveness of your business by highlighting unique selling points, such as strong customer relationships or proprietary technology.

   - Consider timing the sale strategically to capitalize on market trends and demand.

What steps should I take to prepare my business for sale?

- Organize and update financial records, including tax returns, profit and loss statements, and balance sheets.

- Address any operational inefficiencies or outstanding legal issues that could impact the sale process.

- Consider hiring a business broker or advisor to guide you through the preparation process and maximize the value of your business.

How long will it take to sell my business?

- The timeline for selling a business can vary depending on factors such as market conditions, industry dynamics, and the complexity of the transaction.

- On average, the sale process can take several months to a year or more from initial preparation to closing the deal.

- Be prepared for potential delays and fluctuations in the timeline, and work closely with your advisors to navigate any challenges that arise.

How do I find qualified buyers for my business?

- Utilize a multi-channel marketing approach to reach potential buyers, including online listings, industry publications, and networking events.

- Consider engaging with business brokers or M&A advisors who have extensive networks and experience connecting sellers with qualified buyers.

- Screen potential buyers carefully to ensure they have the financial resources and expertise to complete the transaction successfully.

What are the tax implications of selling my business?

- Consult with tax professionals to understand the tax implications of selling your business, including capital gains taxes, depreciation recapture, and potential tax planning strategies.

- Consider structuring the sale in a tax-efficient manner, such as utilizing installment sales or qualified small business stock exemptions, to minimize tax liabilities.

- Be aware of any changes to tax laws or regulations that may impact the sale process and seek guidance accordingly.

How can I ensure confidentiality during the sale process?

- Implement confidentiality measures, such as non-disclosure agreements (NDAs), to protect sensitive information about your business.

- Limit the dissemination of information to only essential parties involved in the sale process, such as qualified buyers and advisors.

- Emphasize the importance of discretion and professionalism to all parties involved and monitor compliance with confidentiality agreements closely.

What role will I play in the sale process?

- Your role as the seller will vary depending on the specific circumstances of the sale and your preferences.

- You may be actively involved in marketing the business, negotiating with potential buyers, and facilitating due diligence, or you may prefer to delegate these tasks to advisors.

- Communicate your expectations and preferences with your advisors and establish clear lines of communication to ensure a smooth and successful sale process.

How can I protect the interests of my employees during the sale?

- Communicate openly and transparently with employees about the sale process, addressing any concerns or questions they may have.

- Consider including provisions in the sale agreement to protect the interests of employees, such as retention bonuses or severance packages.

- Work closely with your advisors to develop a transition plan that minimizes disruptions to employee morale and ensures a smooth handover of responsibilities to the new owner.

What happens after the sale is completed?

- Be prepared for a period of transition following the sale, during which you may need to assist the new owner with integrating the business into their operations.

- Consider your own post-sale plans and objectives, such as retirement or pursuing new business opportunities, and communicate these with your advisors.

- Stay informed about any ongoing obligations or commitments related to the sale, such as consulting agreements or non-compete clauses, and ensure compliance as necessary.

Chapter 5

Bank and Financing Options

Bank financing is a critical component of business sales, offering opportunities for both sellers and buyers to facilitate transactions. Various financing options are available, including traditional term loans, lines of credit, and Small Business Administration (SBA) loans. However, the availability of financing depends on factors such as the buyer's creditworthiness, the business's financial performance, and the terms of the sale agreement. Banks typically evaluate the buyer's creditworthiness, considering factors such as credit history, collateral, and business plans. Collateral may be required to secure financing, such as real estate, equipment, or inventory.

Seller financing can complement bank financing and make transactions more attractive to buyers, especially if they have limited access to traditional bank loans. The Small Business Administration (SBA) offers loan programs specifically designed to support small business acquisitions, providing favorable terms and lower down payment requirements for buyers. However, securing bank financing can impact the sale timeline, as it may take time to complete the loan application, underwriting, and approval process. Sellers and buyers should factor in potential delays associated with bank financing when planning the sale timeline.

Negotiating financing terms with banks is crucial for securing the most favorable terms and conditions. Key terms to consider include interest rates, repayment schedules, loan amounts, and collateral requirements. Sellers and buyers should also assess the risks associated with financing the sale, such as the potential for default or non-payment by the buyer. Seeking professional guidance from financial advisors, business brokers, and legal experts is essential for navigating the complexities of bank financing for business sales. With careful planning and professional assistance, sellers and buyers can leverage bank financing to successfully complete transactions and achieve their goals.

Banks are invaluable partners in assisting sellers throughout the business sale process, offering expertise and guidance to navigate financing options and secure the best deals. They educate sellers on the various financing options available, assess the financial viability of their businesses, and offer competitive financing packages tailored to their needs. By providing guidance on documentation and assisting with the application process, banks help sellers streamline the financing process and maximize their chances of securing funding.

Furthermore, banks negotiate financing terms with sellers to ensure they secure the most favorable deals, considering factors such as interest rates, loan amounts, and repayment schedules. They also collaborate with other professionals involved in the sale process, such as attorneys and accountants, to ensure a coordinated approach and smooth transaction. Throughout the process, banks provide ongoing support to sellers, keeping them informed about the status of their loan applications and offering advice to address any concerns or challenges.

Additionally, banks tailor solutions to the unique circumstances of each business sale, providing creative financing arrangements and advising on risk management strategies. They support sellers in conducting due diligence on potential buyers and facilitate smooth transactions by coordinating financing activities and disbursing funds promptly upon closing. Even after the sale is completed, banks continue to support sellers with post-sale financial management and investment planning, ensuring a long-term partnership that extends beyond the transaction. Overall, banks serve as trusted advisors and partners, helping sellers achieve their financial objectives and maximize the value of their businesses in the sale process.

Chapter 6

Common pitfalls when selling the Business

Navigating the intricate process of selling a business can be fraught with challenges, and sellers often encounter common pitfalls and mistakes that can hinder their success. One prevalent issue is the tendency for sellers to overvalue their businesses, leading to unrealistic asking prices that deter potential buyers. It's crucial for sellers to conduct a comprehensive valuation and market analysis to set a realistic price reflective of the business's true worth.

Furthermore, inadequate preparation can significantly impede the sale process. Sellers must ensure that their financial records are meticulously organized, legal documentation is in order, and the business is presented in its best possible light to attract buyers. Failing to prepare adequately can result in delays, complications, and potentially lower offers from interested parties.

Another common pitfall is the limited marketing efforts employed by sellers. Many underestimate the importance of marketing their business effectively to reach qualified buyers. Utilizing multiple channels such as online listings, industry networks, and engaging with business brokers can significantly broaden the reach and visibility of the sale, increasing the likelihood of finding the right buyer.

Confidentiality is paramount during the sale process to safeguard the business's reputation and prevent disruptions to operations. Sellers must implement strict confidentiality measures, such as non-disclosure agreements, and exercise caution when disclosing sensitive information to serious, qualified buyers.

Emotional attachment to the business can cloud sellers' judgment and hinder negotiation efforts. It's essential for sellers to approach the sale process with objectivity and focus on achieving the best outcome for both parties, rather than allowing emotions to dictate decisions.

Negotiation flexibility is crucial, as sellers who are rigid or inflexible risk alienating potential buyers and jeopardizing the sale. Approaching negotiations with an open mind and willingness to compromise on certain terms can lead to a mutually beneficial agreement.

Ignoring legal and regulatory compliance can result in legal disputes and liabilities for sellers. Adhering to legal requirements throughout the sale process, including contracts, leases, permits, licenses, and employee agreements, is essential to mitigate risks and ensure a smooth transaction.

Insufficient due diligence on potential buyers can lead to issues such as financing challenges or incompatible business philosophies. Sellers should perform thorough due diligence on buyers' financial capabilities, intentions, and reputations to minimize risks and ensure a successful transaction.

Proper management of the transition period post-sale is crucial to minimize disruptions to business operations and maintain employee morale and customer relationships. Sellers should develop a detailed transition plan addressing key aspects such as employee retention, customer communication, and operational continuity to facilitate a smooth transition under new ownership.

Lastly, rushing the process can lead to oversights, mistakes, and suboptimal outcomes. Sellers should take the time to thoroughly vet potential buyers, negotiate favorable terms, and ensure all necessary preparations are in place for a successful transaction. By being aware of these common pitfalls and mistakes, sellers can proactively address them and navigate the business sale process more effectively, increasing their chances of achieving a successful and profitable transaction.

Avoiding costly errors and maximizing success in the business sale process requires careful planning and strategic execution. Starting early is crucial to allow ample time for due diligence, valuation, and marketing efforts. Rushing the process increases the likelihood of errors and compromises. Seeking professional guidance from experienced professionals such as business brokers, attorneys, accountants, and financial advisors can provide valuable insights and expertise to navigate the complexities of the sale process. Their guidance can help sellers avoid pitfalls and optimize outcomes.

Conducting thorough due diligence on your own business is essential to identify any potential issues or liabilities that could deter buyers. Addressing these issues proactively can prevent costly surprises during negotiations. Setting a realistic asking price based on market trends, financial performance, and industry comparables is crucial. Overvaluing or undervaluing the business can have negative consequences, so pricing realistically is key to attracting qualified buyers.

Ensuring that financial records are accurate, up-to-date, and well-organized is paramount.

Potential buyers will scrutinize your financials, so having clean and transparent documentation instills confidence and facilitates negotiations. Implementing strict confidentiality measures to protect sensitive information about the business is critical. Limiting disclosures to serious, qualified buyers and requiring non-disclosure agreements safeguard proprietary data.

Investing in comprehensive marketing efforts to reach a broad audience of potential buyers is essential. Utilizing multiple channels, including online listings, industry networks, and targeted outreach, maximizes exposure and attracts qualified buyers. Approaching negotiations with an open mind and being willing to compromise on certain terms to reach a mutually beneficial agreement is important. Flexibility and collaboration can help overcome obstacles and facilitate successful transactions.

Recognizing and managing any emotional attachment to the business is crucial. Emotions can cloud judgment and hinder negotiations, so maintaining objectivity and focusing on the business's best interests is essential. Developing a detailed transition plan ensures a smooth handover of the business to the new owner. Considering factors such as employee retention, customer communication, and operational continuity minimizes disruptions and maximizes the likelihood of a successful transition.

Staying informed about market trends, regulatory changes, and industry developments is important. Adapting strategies accordingly and making informed decisions throughout the process enhances the chances of success. Finally, following through on all aspects of the sale agreement ensures a seamless closing and successful transition of ownership. By following these practical tips and strategies, sellers can avoid costly errors, mitigate risks, and maximize their chances of achieving a successful and profitable business sale.

Conclusion

In wrapping up this comprehensive guide, let's reflect on the incredible journey you've embarked on in selling your business. It's been a journey filled with ups and downs, challenges, and triumphs. But through it all, you've shown remarkable perseverance, dedication, and a relentless drive to succeed.

As you close this chapter and prepare to turn the page to a new one, remember the invaluable lessons you've learned along the way. From meticulously preparing your business for sale to navigating the complexities of negotiations, you've embraced every step of the process with determination and resilience.

But selling a business isn't just about securing the highest sale price—it's about laying the groundwork for a smooth transition, ensuring the well-being of your employees, and leaving behind a legacy you can be proud of. It's about celebrating the journey you've traveled and the impact you've made on your industry and community.

As you move forward, may you carry with you the wisdom gained from this experience, the relationships nurtured, and the confidence to embrace new opportunities that lie ahead. Remember to lean on the expertise of professionals, stay adaptable in the face of change, and never lose sight of your vision for the future.

So here's to you, the courageous entrepreneur who dared to dream big and took the necessary steps to turn those dreams into reality. May your next chapter be filled with even greater success, fulfillment, and joy. Cheers to your continued journey of growth, prosperity, and making a difference in the world.

86

Leaving a Review

Dear Reader,

I hope this message reaches you well. I deeply appreciate your decision to explore the contents of this book. Our shared journey has been remarkable, and my sincere wish is that you found the book informative and valuable.

As an Author, your feedback means a lot to me. I would greatly appreciate it if you could take a moment to share your thoughts and impressions by leaving a review on the platform where you acquired the book.

Your review is not only valuable feedback for me but also assists other readers in finding the book, enabling them to gauge its relevance to their preferences. Whether you provide a brief summary or a detailed reflection, your honest feedback is highly appreciated. Thank you for joining me on this journey through literature. I look forward to hearing your thoughts and sincerely appreciate the time and thoughtfulness you dedicate to it.

Warm regards,
Lane J. Taylor

www.ingramcontent.com/pod-product-compliance
Lightning Source LLC
Chambersburg PA
CBHW070349230526
45471CB00006B/2488